SPY

GIZMOS

and

Gadgets

BY

SUSAN K. MITCHELL

THE SECRET WORLD OF SPIES

Enslow Publishers, Inc.
40 Industrial Road
Box 398
Berkeley Heights, NJ 07922
USA   http://www.enslow.com

For my wonderful parents, Robbie & Dub

Library of Congress Cataloging-in-Publication Data

Mitchell, Susan K.
    Spy gizmos and gadgets / Susan K. Mitchell.
       p. cm. — (The secret world of spies)
    Includes bibliographical references and index.
    Summary: "Discusses different gadgets used by spies, such as invisible ink, hidden cameras, small
       guns made to look like ordinary objects, and bugs, and includes career information"—Provided by
       publisher.
    ISBN 978-0-7660-3710-6
    1. Espionage—Equipment and supplies—Juvenile literature. 2. Electronic surveillance—Juvenile
       literature. 3. Espionage—Juvenile literature. I. Title.
    UB270.5.M58 2011
    327.12—dc22

                        2010006177

Paperback ISBN 978-1-59845-354-6

Printed in China

052011 Leo Paper Group, Heshan City, Guangdong, China

10 9 8 7 6 5 4 3 2 1

To Our Readers: We have done our best to make sure all Internet Addresses in this book were active and appropriate when we went to press. However, the author and the publisher have no control over and assume no liability for the material available on those Internet sites or on other Web sites they may link to. Any comments or suggestions can be sent by e-mail to comments@enslow.com or to the address on the back cover.

Illustration Credits: Bloomberg / Getty Images, p. 41; Cristian Matei / © iStockphoto.com, p. 20; David Mdzinarishvili / Reuters / Landov, p. 11; Courtesy of the International Spy Museum, pp. 12, 24, 26, 28, 40; Jeffrey Coolidge / Getty Images, p. 32; © Jens Benninghofen / Alamy, p. 15; Library of Congress, p. 9; © Mary Evans Picture Library / Alamy, p. 7; Courtesy of Minox, p. 17; Peter Arnold Images / Photolibrary, p. 37; Reuters / Landov, pp. 23, 31; Shutterstock.com, pp. 3, 4, 35, 39, 42, 44; Time & Life Pictures / Getty Images, p. 33.

Cover Illustration: Mehau Kulyk / Photo Researchers, Inc. (background); Shutterstock.com (camera with zoom lens, lower right corner).

CONTENTS

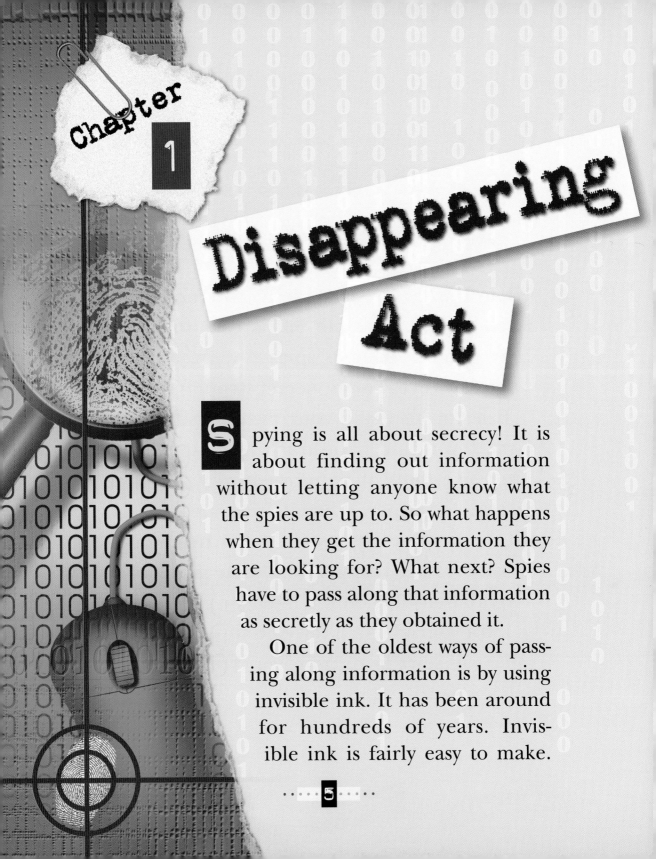

Chapter 1

Disappearing Act

Spying is all about secrecy! It is about finding out information without letting anyone know what the spies are up to. So what happens when they get the information they are looking for? What next? Spies have to pass along that information as secretly as they obtained it.

One of the oldest ways of passing along information is by using invisible ink. It has been around for hundreds of years. Invisible ink is fairly easy to make.

Spying Is as Close as Your Kitchen

When life gives you lemons, why not make invisible ink! Invisible ink is easy to make. This gadget can help spies when they have run out of every other secret weapon.

It is fun to make your own invisible ink. First, dip a thin paintbrush in lemon juice. Then use the wet paintbrush to write your message on paper. When it dries, the message will be completely invisible. To make your secret message reappear, hold the paper over a lightbulb. Turn on the light. Be careful not to burn yourself. In a few minutes, the lemon juice will start to turn brown. Your message will appear!

How do you make invisible ink reappear? Using heat is one of the best ways. Place the paper over a device that gives off heat—a lightbulb or stove top—and the message will begin to show.

Lemon juice, milk, or even urine has been used in the past to send disappearing messages. In more recent times, the recipes for invisible ink have become more complicated.

For a spy, invisible ink is not difficult to use. Messages can be sent on just about anything using the ink. Seemingly ordinary items could possibly be used to send secret messages. It is one of the ultimate gadgets for any spy.

The First American Spy Ring

The American Revolution was the setting for the first American spy ring. A spy ring is a group of spies all working together toward the same goal. The Culper Ring was very important in helping the United States win its war for independence against the British. Spying was a huge part of General George Washington's battle plans. At the heart of the ring was Samuel Culper.

In reality, Samuel Culper did not actually exist. The Culper family was not a true family at all. The members were not even related. They were a group of spies working for Washington against the British. To protect their identity, they used code names. Samuel Culper was one of them.

One of their favorite spy tools was invisible ink. Many of the messages were sent to General Washington using ink that needed heat to make them appear. This type of ink worked well, but the enemy could read the message if they captured it. The American resistance needed a better invisible ink if their spying was going to work.

Spying was an important part of George Washington's battle plans. He helped start the first American spy ring. Washington (center) is depicted here after a victory at the Battle of Trenton during the Revolutionary War.

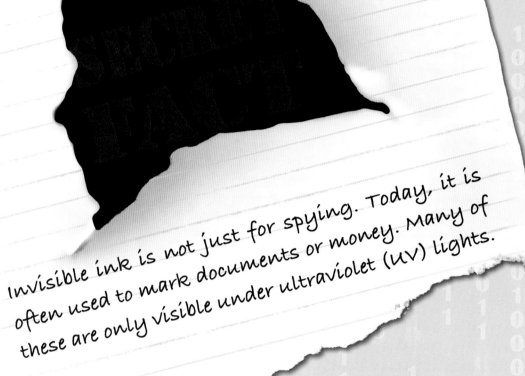

SECRET FACT

Invisible ink is not just for spying. Today, it is often used to mark documents or money. Many of these are only visible under ultraviolet (UV) lights.

Getting the Message

Washington knew that spying was a dangerous business. If caught by the British, it meant death for the spy. He made sure that his patriot spies had the resources they needed to carry out his plans.

Sir James Jay, the brother of patriot John Jay, developed a new invisible ink, often called the "sympathetic stain." It used one chemical to write the message. Another chemical was used to make

it reappear. This was more complicated than other simpler invisible ink recipes.

Washington knew this was a better way to pass secret messages. Even if the British captured the message, they would not be able to read it. Past inks only needed heat to make the message appear. The "stain" would not appear under heat. The British would have needed the second chemical to discover the message.

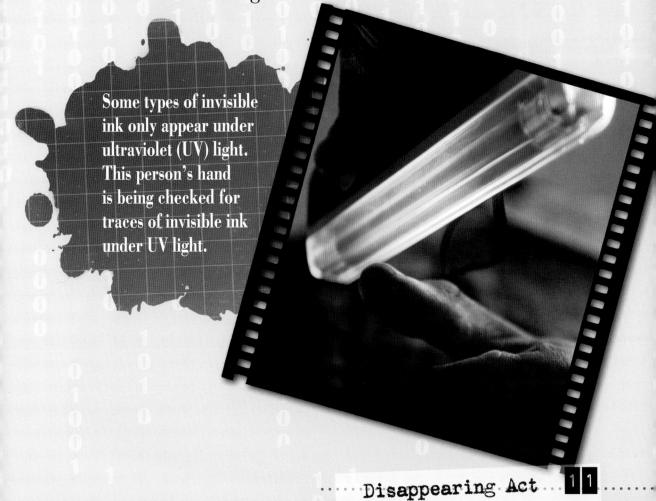

Some types of invisible ink only appear under ultraviolet (UV) light. This person's hand is being checked for traces of invisible ink under UV light.

This is a letter from George Washington requesting that a spy network be created for the Continental army. He wrote the letter in 1777, and the Culper Ring was soon formed. Spies in the Culper Ring had to be very secretive when they passed messages.

Spying Can Be Skin Deep

Invisible ink is useful because it can be written on almost anything. Common items can suddenly become spy documents. During times of war, many creative ways were used to send invisible ink messages.

One German spy even used her own skin! In World War I, the Belgian woman was arrested for spying for the Germans. She was found to have a message written on her back. She was executed.

Spies were instructed by Washington to use invisible ink—or the "stain"—on everyday items like pamphlets, almanacs, and books. His Culper spies sent many messages on the movements and locations of British troops. Their invisible messages were a huge help in winning America's independence.

2

Get the Picture?

Sometimes spies need to figure out the big picture. They need to pass along more information than can be written down. That is when a camera comes in handy. However, spies cannot carry around a clunky camera when they are undercover. They have to use special gadgets, especially for their secret work.

Hidden cameras are nothing new. We see them on television all the time. Perhaps it is a camera catching a thief in the act of robbing a store. It might be an undercover news report. Spies need something just a bit more secretive. They need equipment that can be easily hidden. A camera has to be extremely small in order to get the job done.

It also helps if the camera can be hidden in everyday objects. Spies have to be able to take a picture without blowing their cover. These tiny cameras might look like a pen, a lighter, or a key chain. But really, they are able to take high-quality pictures quickly and quietly. This is an important tool for spies.

The best spy cameras are ones that can be hidden in everyday objects. This button spy camera was hidden in a coat or shirt.

Worth a Thousand Words

One of the most famous spy cameras in history is the Minox camera. Unlike many spy cameras, the Minox actually looks like a camera. It is not disguised as an ordinary object. It is extremely small and easily hidden, however. This tiny camera can fit into the palm of your hand.

The Minox was one of the most widely used spy cameras in the world. During the Cold War with the Soviet Union, however, a better alternative was found: the T-100 camera. The T-100 combined the quality of the Minox with the ability to be hidden in everyday objects.

It became a powerful weapon in the hands of spy Aleksandr Ogorodnik (o-gor-OD-nik). He was a Russian economist who agreed to work for the Central Intelligence Agency (CIA). His code name was Trigon. The CIA trained him to use many tools, the most important being the T-100 camera.

When It All Clicks

The T-100 camera was less than a quarter of the size of the Minox camera. It had a circular shape

SECRET FACT

The first Minox camera was invented by Walter Zapp in 1936. Today, the Minox company makes many different styles of cameras.

that fit easily into objects. It could fit into a pen or a watch. The camera used special ultra-thin film.

Trigon was trained for weeks on how to use the camera properly. To get the best picture, he had to stand exactly eleven inches away from whatever he

Funny Money

Some spies use what are called microdot cameras. These cameras store the secret information they capture on very tiny film called microdots. These dots of film are about one millimeter in diameter. That is about the size of a pencil lead!

Microdots can be hidden in many small places. One favorite place is in hollowed-out coins. On the outside, they look like regular quarters or nickels. These coins often had a backup plan to prevent the wrong person from opening them. They might contain a small amount of acid. If opened incorrectly, the acid would destroy the microdot film.

Trigon was eventually discovered and captured by the Russian KGB. He committed suicide by swallowing a cyanide pill during questioning.

was photographing. He also had to learn to make it look completely natural. It had to look like he was NOT taking a picture.

He became so good at using the T-100 that he decided to go on a mission before his training was complete. Trigon was able to snap shots of secret Soviet documents while he was in Colombia. The camera was delivered to a CIA agent. Then it was sent to Washington, D.C. Almost every picture was clear and readable! This helped give the CIA an advantage in the Cold War.

Satellite cameras have become important gadgets to spy agencies.

Spies in the Sky

Not all cameras can fit in your hand. In fact, some cameras are out of this world. Literally! They are located on spy satellites in outer space. These cameras are able to zoom in at amazing distances to take pictures.

Some of these satellite cameras can take pictures of objects as small as three feet wide. A special few can even see images as small as three inches wide! That is amazing because they are often hundreds of miles above Earth.

Chapter 3

No Ordinary Weapons

The main goal for spies is to gather secrets. Their job is not usually to kill anyone. Very rarely do they have to use a weapon. But where there is danger, there may be a need for them. So spies need to have weapons that are easily hidden and easily used.

Weapons have two basic uses. One use is for defense. A spy may have to fight for his or her life if discovered. These weapons could be a small, hidden blade or gun. These might not kill anyone.

However, they can give the spy enough time to escape his or her enemy.

The other use for a weapon is for attack. There are a few spies whose job goes far beyond finding out secrets. They are assassins. Today, assassination is illegal in the United States. But assassins are still operating today in many parts of the world. Their job is to hunt down their targets and eliminate them. Their weapons can often be much more complicated than defensive weapons.

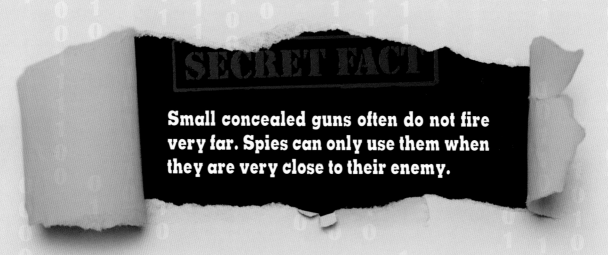

SECRET FACT

Small concealed guns often do not fire very far. Spies can only use them when they are very close to their enemy.

When It Rains, It Poisons

September 7, 1978, started like an ordinary day for Georgi Markov. He was a Bulgarian novelist and reporter living in London. Markov was very outspoken against the government of his home

Georgi Markov's writing and radio reports made him many enemies in his home country of Bulgaria.

country of Bulgaria. His writing and radio reports had made him many enemies.

That day, Markov walked across the Waterloo Bridge in London. He stood waiting for a bus. Then, suddenly, he felt a sharp pain in his leg. As Markov spun around, he saw a man behind him grab an umbrella and rush away. The man was a Bulgarian secret agent and an assassin.

It turns out the umbrella was actually a secret weapon. The inside was similar to an air rifle. The assassin pushed a trigger near the umbrella handle. This activated pressured air to push a small pellet of poison through the tip of the umbrella. The pellet contained a poison called ricin (RY-sin).

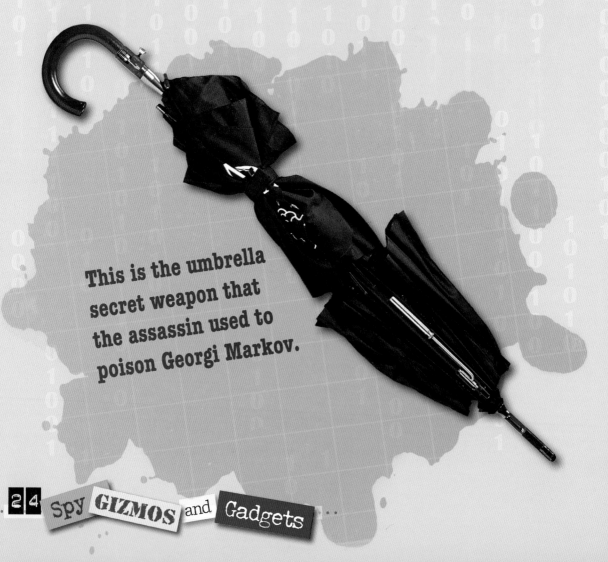

This is the umbrella secret weapon that the assassin used to poison Georgi Markov.

No Plans to Die

The CIA does not often speak openly about plans to kill other country's leaders. However, over the years, attempts to assassinate Cuban leader Fidel Castro have been uncovered.

One of the wildest plots was to poison Castro's beloved cigars. Milk shakes and aspirin were also poisoned in an attempt to kill Castro. The CIA failed in all their attempts to kill the Cuban leader.

It is important to realize that these plans happened before 1976. In that year, it was declared illegal to try and kill another government leader. Since 1976, there have been no documented attempts on Castro's life by the CIA.

SECRET FACT

The Soviet KGB has one weapon called "The Kiss of Death." It was a tube of lipstick designed to fire a single shot.

Situation Unknown

Markov gave the incident little thought. However, the pain in his leg did not go away. By the time he arrived at work, he was in great pain. Within a day, Markov developed a fever and became quite ill. By this time, Markov began to suspect he had been poisoned. He died in the hospital four days after the incident with the mysterious "umbrella man."

After Markov died, his body was taken for investigation. Doctors did find a small pellet imbedded inside his lower leg. It was a tiny metal pellet about the size of a pin. This was what had held the ricin poison.

Unfortunately, Markov's fate had been sealed the minute the assassin shot him with the pellet. Even if doctors had found the pellet early, Markov still would have died. There is no known antidote for ricin poison. As of today, the umbrella killer has never been caught.

No Smoking Please

Today, the health dangers of smoking are well known. Cigarettes can cause severe health problems. In years past, however, smoking was a popular activity. Spies often used this to their advantage.

One weapon used a small tube that looked like a cigarette. It was called the "stinger." It could shoot a single bullet if the spy pulled a small string with his teeth. Another weapon was a pack of cigarettes designed to give off a poison gas in the enemy's face.

Back when smoking was more common, the "stinger" gun was designed to look like a cigarette. Spies could shoot the weapon by pulling a string with their teeth.

Drop Dead Drops

Discovering secrets is only one part of a spy's job. Once the spy has the information he or she needs, the spy has to get it to the right people. Those people are usually called a spy's handlers. Gaining secret information is no good if it is never passed along. This is where a dead drop can come into play.

Dead drops are not as horrible as their name sounds. It is a place for a spy to hide information. The information stays hidden until those working with the spy come to get it. Only the spy and his or her counterpart know the location.

It is important for a dead drop to withstand time and weather. It has to look natural or be well hidden. Often, a dead drop looks like a rock or a log. Other times it is a spike that is waterproof and weatherproof. Still, others may be a hollowed-out brick or book.

SECRET FACT

One spy really put the "dead" in the concept of dead drops. He used a dead rat to pass along important information!

Chalk Marks the Spot

Having the dead drop is only the first step in passing along secrets. A spy must be able to signal to a handler that the drop has been used. A spy needs a way to tell the handler there is information that needs to be picked up. This has to be a secret signal that only the spy and handler know. It may be a light in a certain window or a specific color item placed in a certain spot.

CIA traitor Aldrich Ames used dead drops to give spy information to the Russian KGB. He also used them to pick up money and instructions from the KGB.

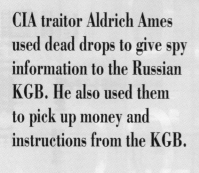

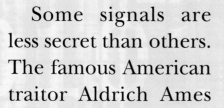

Some signals are less secret than others. The famous American traitor Aldrich Ames used chalk marks as his signal. These marks were made to signal his handlers. Ames was a former CIA worker. He was also working for the Russian KGB. He was stealing CIA secrets and selling them for money.

Ames would leave documents and letters in different dead drops. Some of them were ordinary mailboxes. The KGB would also leave money and instructions for Ames in similar dead drops.

Spying by the Book

SECRET PROJECT

You can make your own simple dead drop. This can be a fun way to pass messages between you and a friend. One way is to create a book safe. You need your parents' help for this.

Create your own dead drop with an old hardcover book. The book can hide secret information or important valuables.

First, find an old hardcover book that no one reads anymore. Flip to about the tenth page. Using a pencil and ruler, draw a rectangle on the right-hand page. Make sure to leave plenty of space around the rectangle. You need to measure more than about an inch from the outer edges of the page.

Have your parents use an Exacto knife to cut along the edge of the rectangle you drew. These knives are very sharp. Do not try to use them yourself. Keep cutting through about half of the book. Eventually you will have a hollowed-out book where you and a friend can pass messages.

Getting the Drop on a Traitor

Ames would often mark his drops with chalk. This would signal his KGB handlers that there was something for them to pick up. This helped protect Ames in later years because he did not have to meet face-to-face with the KGB. It lowered his risk of being caught.

According to the plan, the KGB would erase the mark when they picked up the new information. This did not always go as planned. Ames was frustrated with using the dead drops. His main complaint was that the small size of dead drops limited the amount of money he could get at one time.

By 1993, the Federal Bureau of Investigation (FBI) was following Ames. They were suspicious of

Aldrich Ames used this mailbox, code named "Smile," as a dead drop site in Washington, D.C. He marked the mailbox with chalk to signal a meeting with the KGB.

his activity and had begun to investigate. The FBI found records that showed one dead-drop site was a mailbox at 37th and R streets in Washington, D.C. They began to keep track of his chalk marks. Ames was finally arrested in 1994 and convicted of spying. He is serving a life sentence in prison.

Drops in Cyberspace

The Internet has changed many aspects of spying. One of these changes has been the use of dead drops. In recent years, terrorist cells have been discovered using e-mail accounts as virtual dead drops. This is how it works. A terrorist cell sets up an anonymous e-mail account. All the members share the password. Instead of sending messages, they save the messages as drafts. This keeps the messages from being found by government agencies.

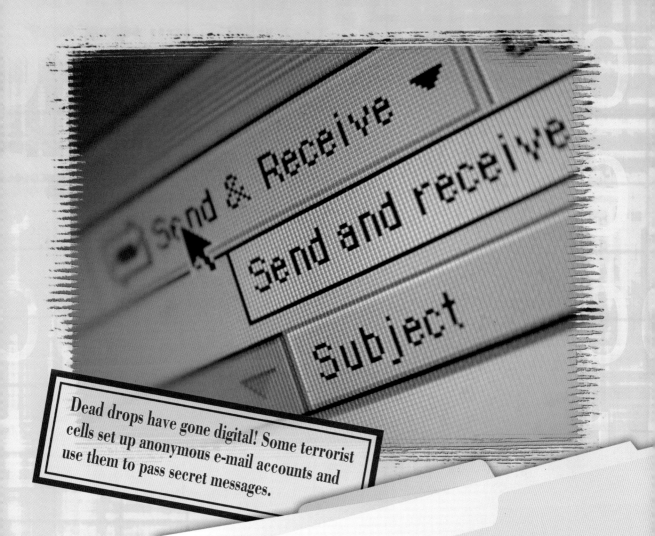

Dead drops have gone digital! Some terrorist cells set up anonymous e-mail accounts and use them to pass secret messages.

SECRET FACT

Dead drops are also sometimes called dead-letter boxes.

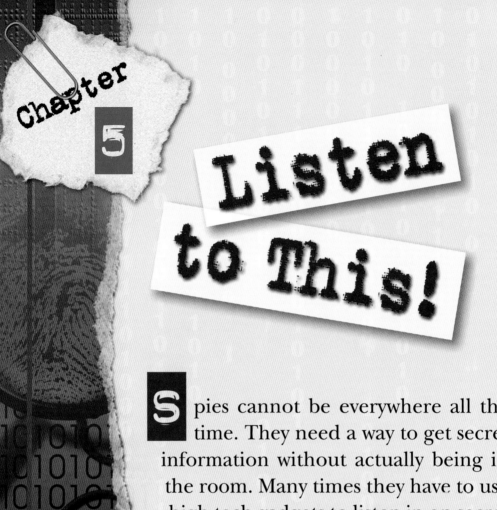

Chapter 5

Listen to This!

Spies cannot be everywhere all the time. They need a way to get secret information without actually being in the room. Many times they have to use high-tech gadgets to listen in on secret conversations. These listening devices are often called bugs.

Bugs are usually very small. Like most spy tools, they can be well hidden in or on everyday objects. They allow a spy to listen in on private situations. Bugs use sensitive microphones. These are attached to a radio transmitter. The spy can stay a safe distance away and still hear every secret whisper.

Listening devices can also be hidden inside a phone. This is often called bugging. Bugs can even be hidden on a person! They can be placed on clothing or even on a spy's body. This is sometimes called "wearing a wire." Whatever it is called, the goal is the same—to get the secrets the spy is searching for.

Sealed Secrets

The United States has long been a leader in the spy game. In the past, however, it has been victim to spying from other agencies. In 1946, Soviet

This photo shows a miniature listening device. Bugs, like this one, can be hidden inside a phone.

Spy agencies are also always inventing ways of finding these listening devices. Debugging tools pick up unusual radio signals. They indicate that a room or object might contain a bug.

schoolchildren presented a beautiful wooden carving of the Great Seal of the United States to an ambassador. He hung the gift over his desk in his Moscow embassy office. The large carved eagle proudly watched over the room.

But it did far more than just watch. Inside the seal was a small bug called the "Thing." It was one of the most sophisticated listening devices of the time. It did not record everything. The Thing could only be activated by an outside source.

Soviet agents would aim a transmitter in the direction of the device. They could do this easily from a parked van near the embassy home. The transmitter would emit radio signals. This would then trigger a slim antenna inside the seal. The microphone would then pick up sounds.

Bugs on the Move

The widespread use of cell phones has added a new twist to using bugs. Special software can send a hidden code to a cell phone. The code acts a bit like a virus. This can trigger a cell phone to work just like a microphone. It is similar to hacking a computer.

Cell phones can also be used as tracking devices. Many of them have a built in GPS (global positioning system). This allows satellites to show the user's exact location.

oviet schoolchildren gave the Great Seal of the United States (at left in glass case) to the U.S. ambassador in Moscow. But the seal had a hidden listening device inside it. The Great Seal is now on display at the International Spy Museum in Washington, D.C.

Squishing the Bug

It seemed like the perfect bug. Because it was activated from outside, it was almost impossible to detect by debugging tools. For six years, the Great Seal bug hung in the embassy office. It recorded an unknown number of secret conversations. Not until 1952 was the bug finally discovered.

The Great Seal bug remained inside the embassy office for six years before it was discovered. Listening devices are great spying gadgets. In Rome, Italy, this private investigator uses a device that can determine if a phone is being tapped.

It is illegal to listen in on or record private conversations. Only authorized police or government agents can legally use bugs. Even then, they must have a very good reason for doing so.

This is a vintage reel-to-reel recording device. Only law enforcement and government agencies can legally record private conversations.

A British radio operator overheard conversations from the U.S. Embassy in Moscow. American agencies searched the embassy from top to bottom. They finally figured out that it was hidden in the large wooden carving of the Great Seal.

There are no estimates of how many secrets may have been discovered by the Soviet spies. Over time, more than one hundred other bugs were found hidden in similar seals in U.S. embassies. If the Thing had not been discovered in 1952, it might still be working even today.

SPIES Like Who?

A CAREER IN GADGETS

Ever have an idea for a great spy gadget? If so, then a job at the Office of Technical Services (OTS) might be for you. It might sound like a boring place to work. However, the OTS is the branch of the CIA that creates amazing spy equipment. Whatever gadget a spy may need, the research scientists and engineers at the OTS can design it.

The OTS gadget gurus often have college degrees in engineering or mathematics. Many of them have either a master's degree or a PhD. Others have degrees in chemistry or physics. Salaries for an OTS research scientist can range from $60,000 to more than $100,000 per year.

Are you interested in working with amazing gadgets? A career in the Office of Technical Services (OTS) would give you that opportunity. But to work with cool spy equipment, you must have good skills in math and computers and have an interest in engineering.

Glossary

ambassador—A person who acts as a country's representative in foreign lands.

assassinate—To kill suddenly or secretively.

economist—A person who studies the economy.

handler—A person who acts as a mediator between a spy and an agency.

resistance—A group of people working against a country or government.

traitor—A person who betrays his or her country or government.

To Find Out More

Books

De Winter, James. **Amazing Tricks of Real Spies.** Mankato, Minn.: Capstone Press, 2010.

Earnest, Peter, and Suzanne Harper, in association with the Spy Museum. **The Real Spy's Guide to Becoming a Spy.** New York: Abrams Books for Young Readers, 2009.

Kelley, K. C. **How Spies Work.** Mankato, Minn.: Smart Apple Media, 2009.

Martin, Michael. **Spy Gear.** Mankato, Minn.: Capstone Press, 2008.

Rauf, Don. **Killer Lipstick and Other Spy Gadgets.** New York: Franklin Watts, 2008.

Timblin, Stephen. **Spy Technology.** Mankato, Minn.: Smart Apple Media, 2010.

Internet Addresses

Central Intelligence Agency (CIA): Kids' Page
 <https://www.cia.gov/kids-page/index.html>

The International Spy Museum: Games and
 Activities
 <http://www.spymuseum.org/kids/games>

Spy Letters of the American Revolution
 <http://www2.si.umich.edu/spies/>

Index